JEWEL BEETLE
CHECKERED BEETLE
FEATHER WINGED BEETLE
PIE DISH BEETLE
DIVING BEETLE
HORNED BEETLE
TOE WINGED BEETLE
SCREECH BEETLE
SAP BEETLE
TEXAS BEETLE
HAIRY FUNGUS BEETLE
SOLDIER BEETLE
PLEASING FUNGUS BEETLE
LONGHORN BEETLE
PEG BEETLE
FIDDLER BEETLE
RAINBOW STAG BEETLE

Because, for always. For Ayana. R.W.

For Maryann and Donna, thank you. H.P. & M.J.

Thank you to the staff at Bayside Libraries.

First published in 2024 by

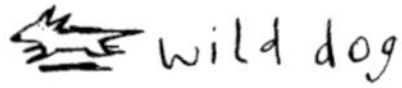

wdog.com.au
Melbourne, Australia

A catalogue record for this book is available from the National Library of Australia

ISBN: 9781742036656 (hbk)

Printed and bound by Everbest Ltd

10 9 8 7 6 5 4 3 2 1    24 25 26 27 28 29

The Illustrations in this book were painted with watercolours.

# One little dung beetle

Rhiân Williams

with illustrations by

Heather Potter & Mark Jackson

1

One little dung beetle
rolling up some poo,
working very hard,
like a beetle likes to do.

# 2

Two black rhino beetles
meeting in the bush,
one beetle nudges
and the other gives a push.

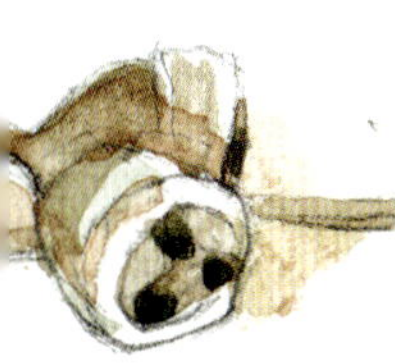

3

Three bold Christmas beetles
buzzing at the door,
tapping most insistently,
then falling to the floor.

4

Four squeaky screech beetles
piping up a sound,
hidden in the mud,
drumming deeply in the ground.

# 5

Five rainbow stag beetles
zooming through the sky,
with a flash and a glint,
they sparkle as they fly.

Six shiny peg beetles
nesting in a stump,
feeding all their babies,
until they're round and plump.

7

Seven skinny click beetles
flipping through the air,
some are over here
and the others over there.

8

Eight hungry diving beetles
hunting for a feed.
Will they spot the tiny tadpoles
hiding in the weed?

9

Nine green fiddler beetles
marching on a track,
noses in the air,
and the smallest at the back.

10

Ten feather horned beetles
climbing through the trees,
peeping through the twigs,
their horns waving in the breeze.

How many beetles?
Beetles galore.
So many beetles,
they're hard to ignore.

Too many beetles,
that's for sure.
So let's stop counting
before there's more.

## Beetles are found on every continent except Antarctica.

A beetle starts as an egg, which hatches into a larva then grows to a pupa before finally becoming a beetle. These changes are known as metamorphosis.

**RHINOCEROS BEETLES** can lift up to 850 times their own body weight. This makes them one of the strongest animals on the planet.

**PEG BEETLES** live in colonies where the adult beetles cooperate to take care of the eggs, larvae and pupae.

**RAINBOW STAG BEETLES** live in the tropical rainforest of Far North Queensland. The male beetles have fierce-looking jaws.

**CLICK BEETLES** make a clicking sound by manipulating their body and catapulting into the air. If click beetles get tipped upside down, they can click and flip themselves the right way up.

# Beetle facts

Beetles have a hard pair of forewings called elytra which help to protect the fragile hindwings they use to fly.

**CHRISTMAS BEETLES**
are attracted to light. Their favourite food is gum leaves.

**SCREECH BEETLES**
make noise by rubbing the hard shell that covers their wings against their abdomens.

**DUNG BEETLES**
There are more than 5000 species of dung beetles found around the world. The world's largest dung beetle is found in Africa. Australian dung beetles are fussy about the type of poo they like to eat. Some will only eat the poo of kangaroos and wallabies.

**DIVING BEETLES**
trap air bubbles underneath the hard covers over their wings. They breathe this trapped air while hunting for tadpoles and small fish.

**FIDDLER BEETLES**
can be green or yellow. They look like they have a violin on their back. Fiddler beetles eat the nectar from flowers.

**FEATHER HORNED BEETLES**
are found all over Australia. Their wing covers are marked with white spots.

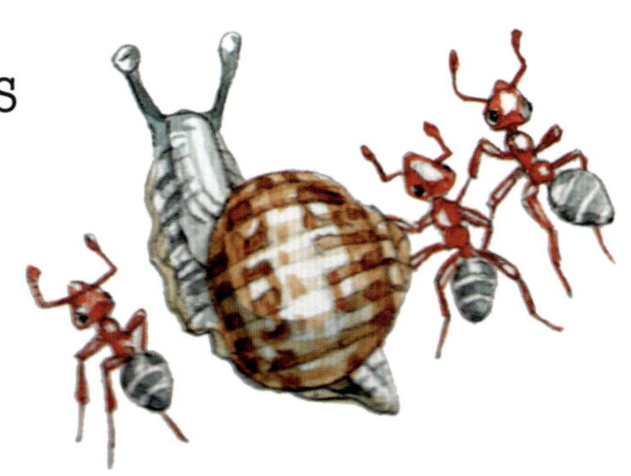

DUNG BEETLE
BOMBARDIER BEETLE
IRON CLAD BEETLE
DARKLING BEETLE
LEAF BEETLE
ORCHID BEETLE
LADYBIRD
WATER PENNY BEETLE
WHIRLYGIG BEETLE
FLAT BARK BEETLE
TORTOISE BEETLE
TUMBLING FLOWER BEETLE
RHINOCEROS BEETLE
CHRISTMAS BEETLE
CLICK BEETLE